The Thrill of Racing

NICKI CLAUSEN-GRACE

Rourke
Publishing LLC
Vero Beach, Florida 32964

www.rourkepublishing.com

PHOTO CREDITS: © Library of Congress: page 5; ©David Ferroni: page 6; © Graham Bloomfield: page 7; © JACK BRADEN: page 8; © Chrysler Media: page 8; © Bryan Eastham: page 9; © Scott Scheibelhut: page 10; © GM Racing Photo: page 12, 16, 22; © Todd Taulman: page 11, 12, 21; © Kevin Norris: page 14; © Arlo Abrahamson: page 16; © bsankow: page 17; ©Honda Media: page 18

Edited by Meg Greve

Cover design by Tara Raymo
Interior design by Teri Intzegian

Library of Congress Cataloging-in-Publication Data

Library of Congress Cataloging-in-Publication Data

Clausen-Grace, Nicki.
 Sprint car racing / Nicki Clausen-Grace.
   p. cm. -- (The thrill of racing)
 Includes index.
 ISBN 978-1-60472-377-9
 1. Automobile racing--Juvenile literature. 2. Sprint cars--Juvenile
literature. I. Title.
 GV1029.9.S67C53 2009
 796.72--dc22

                      2008011248

Rourke Publishing

www.rourkepublishing.com – rourke@rourkepublishing.com
Post Office Box 3328. Vero Beach. FL 32964

Table of Contents

The World of Outlaws

Would you have much confidence in a car that needed a push to start? Drivers in the World of Outlaws racing series do not have a problem with it. They race **winged sprint cars** on a dirt track and once they get going, these cars can move! The World of Outlaws is a **racing series**, or set of races that take place all over the U.S. from February through November.

Winged sprint cars may start slow but they can go more than 150 mph (241 km/h).

In a racing series, drivers **accumulate**, or gather points for each race they win throughout the year. Whoever has the most points at the end of the year wins the series. Some drivers see World of Outlaws as a way to get into NASCAR (National Association for Stock Car Auto Racing). Jeff Gordon, Tony Stewart, Kraig Kinser, and Kasey Kahne are all NASCAR drivers who first raced in World of Outlaws.

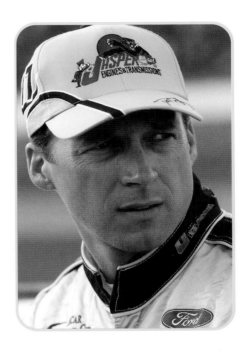

Dave Blaney got his start in the World of Outlaws. He was the 1995 series champion. Now he races in NASCAR in the Nextel cup and Busch series.

In the 1970s, sprint car drivers went around the country racing where they could. They did not have races specifically for their class of cars and sometimes had trouble finding places to run.

Ted Johnson helped make sprint car racing more popular by starting The World of Outlaws racing series.

Ted Johnson started the World of Outlaws racing series because he wanted sprint car racers to have a place to race and a guaranteed **purse**. Since then the series has grown to 85 races each year with widespread television and newspaper coverage.

Winged sprint cars look like powerfully built go-karts. They must weigh at least 1,375 pounds (624 kilograms) including the driver. The 410 cubic inch (6,719 cubic centimeters) engine burns methanol, a type of simple alcohol. They have a large, square aluminum wing mounted on the top and smaller, rectangular wings mounted above the front wheels. They have to be pushed to start because they do not have a starter or a battery.

Wings on the top measure five feet by five feet (1.5 meters by 1.5 meters).

Wings above the front wheel measure two feet by three feet (.6 meter by .9 meter).

Have you ever played darts? The top wing on a sprint car works like the feathers at the end of a dart. They help keep the car going in the right direction. The driver can adjust these wings as needed.

Wings help the car stay on the ground by producing a **downforce**, a strong air current that forces the wheels down onto the track.

In 1988, the World of Outlaws added another series of races featuring late model sprint cars. These are different from the winged cars. They are full-bodied and built to look like popular cars you might see on the street. They are heavier too, weighing 2,300 pounds (1,430 kilograms).

Late model sprint cars look a little like street cars but you won't see them on the road.

Late model sprint cars do not have wings, but they do drive on dirt. Instead of methanol, they run on regular racing gasoline.

Late model sprint cars slide on dirt too.

The World of Outlaws events follow a predictable sequence. First, all cars must drive a few hot laps to prove they can go fast enough to keep up. Next, there are time trials to determine the **heat** in which drivers will race.

Cars must drive three or more hot laps before the race.

Depending on their time in the trial, drivers will compete in a heat race. Winners of the heat races move on to the main event known as the **A-Feature**. The winner of the A-Feature is the champion for the day, but other drivers get points toward the series title.

Car number 67 speeds to finish at the top of the heat.

The Dirt on Dirt

Many tracks have clay as a base, which workers cover with different kinds of dirt. They sprinkle water on the dirt and run a tractor over it to prepare the track for a race.

Knoxville Raceway in Iowa uses Des Moines black-bottom gumbo dirt on their track.

Dirt keeps races exciting because the drivers slip and slide around corners. Lucky fans sometimes have to dodge flying clay as wheels churn it up.

Watch out for flying dirt!

Racing winged sprint cars can be dangerous, so drivers take precautions to stay safe. They wear full-face helmets, fire suits, and multipoint harnesses.

Drivers dress for success.

The cars have safety features too. Roll bars or cages protect drivers if the car flips over. Reinforced **fuel cells** help keep the gas away from sparks. Some people also say that the wings help keep drivers safe during rollovers.

Roll cages stop the car from crushing the driver.

The series starts in Florida each February at the Volusia Speedway. From there it travels across the nation to places like Eldora Speedway in Ohio, Silver Dollar Speedway in California, Knoxville Raceway in Iowa, and Williams Grove Speedway in Pennsylvania.

The biggest and final event in the series is the Outlaws World Finals at Lowe's Motor Speedway in Concord, North Carolina in November.

Thrilling Fact
The National Sprint Car Hall of Fame and Museum is just two miles from the Knoxville Raceway.

The World of Outlaws series tours the country.

Racing winged sprint cars is not cheap. Cars can cost up to $100,000. Maintaining and transporting a car, paying a crew, and covering travel expenses can cost from $100,000 to $2,000,000 a year. Drivers have **sponsors** who own the cars and pay for expenses.

Wings make a great place for sponsors to advertise.

It pays to win. Single events pay $10,000 to $50,000 to the winner, which drivers split with the car owner and crew. The winner of the whole series will take home an additional $200,000.

Donny Schatz won $450,000 during the 2007 season. He added $200,000 to that total by winning the series for the year.

Winged sprint cars may need a shove to get started, but the fame and money brought to the sport by the World of Outlaws racing series has moved them to the front of motorsports.

Glossary

accumulate (uh-KYOO-myuh-late): to gather or collect

aluminum (hu-LOO-mi-nuhm): a light, silver-colored metal

A-Feature (AY-FEE-chur): the final race of the night which decides who is the overall winner

downforce (DOUN-forss): a strong air current that forces the wheels down onto the track

fuel cells (FYOOL sels): small, reinforced containers that help keep fuel from spilling in an accident

heat (HEET): a practice race

purse (PURSS): the total amount of prize money for an event

racing series (RAYSS-ing SIHR-eez): a set of races where drivers gather points to see who can get the most

sponsors (SPON-sers): people or companies who pay the expenses of a car, driver, and crew and in turn use the car and uniforms to advertise

winged sprint cars (wingd SPRINT cars): small, open wheel racing cars with wings on the top and nose

Index

Websites to Visit

www.jeffgordon.com

www.sarahfisher.com

www.kidzworld.com/quiz/4479-quiz-nascar

Further Reading

O'Leary, Mike. *Outlaw Sprints.* Motorbooks, 2002.

Schaefer, A.R. and Betty Carlan. *Sprint Cars.* Edge Books, 2004.

Sexton, Susan. *Sprint Car Racing: Unleashing the Power.* Perfection
    Learning, 2003.

About the Author

Nicki Clausen-Grace is an author and fourth grade teacher. She lives in Florida where they launch the first World of Outlaws event each year. While she has never driven on dirt, she does enjoy cruising along the beach with her husband Jeff, and two children, Brad and Alexandra.